Michael Thigpen

A Symphony of Code

A Comprehensive Guide to Crafting Music with Artificial Intelligence

Dear Musicians and Music Lovers,

Greetings, everyone! I am beyond thrilled and honored to present this project to you. The journey to bring this creation to life has been filled with challenges, trials, and triumphs, and now, the moment has arrived to share the fruits of this labor with all of you.

As you turn the pages ahead, get ready to embark on a musical odyssey. My sincere hope is that this journey not only challenges the boundaries of your mind and perceptions of music but, most importantly, fills your heart and soul with pure joy.

My name is Michael, and my musical journey has been a lifelong adventure. It all began in my childhood, where I was fortunate enough to grow up with a distinctive perspective on both music and life itself. Throughout the weekdays, the soundtrack of my life consisted of pop and rock tunes, but when the weekends rolled around, I found myself immersed in the authentic world of country music alongside my dad.

As a teenager, my musical tastes naturally evolved towards rock, pulling me into the captivating realm of Bass Guitar, Piano/ Keys, and eventually, the intricate world of the 6-string guitar. This journey has not only shaped my musical skills but has also allowed me to explore the diverse landscapes of music, wanting to embrace each note, to tell a unique story of my experiences and influences.

Ah, my musical learning years—pure old-school vibes. It was all about soaking up knowledge from friends, devouring magazines, and losing myself in videos of talented musicians. Back then, I had no fixed destination in mind, but that didn't bother me one bit. My goal was simple: learn it all, unravel the mysteries of what made music tick, understand the intricacies, especially the elusive secrets hidden within the strings of the guitar.

Fast forward forty years, and what do you know? I'm still on this musical odyssey, eagerly absorbing everything about music that I can lay my hands on. From deciphering notations to exploring the visual journey through photos, and yes, diving headfirst into the marvels of modern Artificial Intelligence technology. Initially hesitant, it struck me—hey, we've been using tech all along, like those trusty 4 tracks and recording equipment.

AI isn't here to replace the magic; it's more like a versatile tool, akin to a killer chorus effect or that soul-soothing reverb. The realization hit me—it's there to lend a helping hand, not take over the stage. It's a companion in this musical expedition, not the maestro, that would be you and I as we control the AI.

With humility, I extend a sharing of my musical knowledge to you. Your time and support are sincerely appreciated, and from the depths of my heart, I wish you nothing but boundless success. My door is perpetually open, and I take great pride in personally responding to emails and phone calls. Feel free to reach out and share your stories anytime by visiting www.thigpenscopywriting.com. Explore the blog and the feedback section, where your thoughts are more than welcome. Looking forward to hearing from you!

Michael Shane Thigpen
support@thigpenscopywriting.com

CHAPTER 1: PRELUDE TO THE FUTURE -

The Harmonic Convergence of AI and Music

In the vast tapestry of human achievement, few intersections are as compelling as the fusion of artificial intelligence (AI) and music. Chapter 1 serves as our prologue, setting the stage for a profound exploration into the intricate world where the seemingly disparate realms of technology and art coalesce into a harmonious symphony. Let us embark on this journey of discovery, where the overture of innovation beckons us into uncharted territories.

The Overture of Understanding:

As we unfurl the curtains to reveal the opening act, it is paramount to grasp the nuances of the overture that precedes the orchestration of AI and music. Artificial Intelligence, a testament to human ingenuity, emerges as a transcendent force, permeating the fabric of our existence. Its integration with music, a timeless expression of human emotion, marks a paradigm shift in the creative landscape.

AI, in its various forms, has become a transformative agent across industries, from healthcare to finance. In the realm of music, it augments creativity, blurring the lines between the creator and the created. This overture sets the tone for a symphony where human artistry and machine intelligence engage in a captivating dance, each influencing the other in a reciprocal embrace.

The Maestros Behind the Curtain:

Our journey into the heart of this synergy unveils the visionary architects orchestrating this grand spectacle. Picture the maestros behind the curtain – composers, programmers, and AI engineers converging to shape the future of musical expression. These modern-day alchemists wield algorithms as instruments, conducting a digital symphony where creativity knows no bounds.

The collaboration between artistic minds and technological virtuoso's births a new breed of creators. These maestros harmonize human intuition with the precision of AI, navigating the uncharted waters of musical possibility. They stand at the forefront of a revolution, crafting a narrative where the dichotomy between the organic and the artificial dissolves.

The Instruments of AI:

In our exploration, it becomes imperative to understand the instruments that AI brings to this musical tableau. Imagine machine learning algorithms as virtuoso performers, trained to decipher the intricate patterns embedded within musical data. These algorithms, akin to seasoned musicians, learn from vast datasets, identifying subtleties and creating a lexicon of musical expressions.

Neural networks, the bedrock of AI's cognitive prowess, play a role akin to virtuoso instrumentalists. They interpret the patterns identified by algorithms, infusing compositions with a depth of emotion and complexity that transcends preconceived notions of machine-generated art. It is through this intricate interplay of algorithms and neural networks that AI becomes a true collaborator in the creative process.

The Dance of Creativity:

Our narrative unfolds as a delicate dance between human composers and their AI counterparts. It is not a rivalry but a symbiotic partnership, a pas de deux where ideas flow seamlessly between creator and machine. Human composers, armed with intuition and emotion, engage with AI systems that bring forth novel perspectives, challenging the boundaries of conventional musicality.

In this dance, AI becomes a conduit for innovation, offering alternative pathways for creative expression. The human touch retains its irreplaceable essence, while the digital partner injects a spark of the unexpected. The resultant compositions are a testament to the beauty that emerges when technology and artistic vision converge.

The Echoes of Generative Art:

Within this narrative, generative art emerges as a prominent protagonist, weaving its threads through the fabric of our exploration. Generative algorithms, a manifestation of AI's generative capacity, autonomously produce music that transcends conventional compositions. These algorithms, akin to avant-garde composers, create pieces that surprise, challenge, and evoke a sense of wonder.

Generative art invites us to ponder the nature of creativity itself. Is it confined to the human mind, or can algorithms give birth to truly innovative, emotionally resonant compositions? The echoes of generative art resound with a resounding "yes," pushing the boundaries of what we consider possible in the realm of musical creation.

Real-world Crescendos:

To ground our theoretical exploration, let us delve into real-world examples that exemplify the marriage of AI and music. The AI-generated album "Hello World," a collaborative venture between Skygge (Benjamin Mouton) and the AI program Flow Machines, stands as a testament to the transformative power of this alliance.

This is an interesting track, explaining flow tracks while giving a great example of AI generated music. Getting your gears

turning......
https://www.youtube.com/watch?v=jPp0jIJvDQs

The Melody of Ethical Considerations:

As we navigate this intricate symphony, it is essential to attune our ears to the undertones of ethical considerations. The marriage of AI and music prompts profound questions about authorship, intellectual property, and the evolving role of the artist. How do we navigate a landscape where the lines between human and machine creativity blur?

The ethical considerations echo like a subtle undertone, challenging us to reflect on the responsible use of AI in the creative process. As we revel in the beauty of this emerging symphony, we must also grapple with the implications of our creations on the ethical compass that guides our collective artistic endeavors.

The Crescendo of Possibilities:

In the grand finale of this chapter, we find ourselves standing on the precipice of endless possibilities. The convergence of AI and music is not merely a technological advancement; it is a cultural metamorphosis. It challenges our perceptions, broadens our understanding of creativity, and invites us to redefine the very essence of what it means to be a creator.

As we conclude this chapter, the symphony of AI and music resonates with a crescendo that heralds a future where the boundaries between human and machine creativity become increasingly porous. We are witnesses to a harmonic convergence that transcends the limitations of tradition, paving the way for a new era in the annals of artistic expression.

The journey has just begun, and the subsequent chapters promise to unravel even more layers of this intricate world where AI and music dance in harmonious unison. Join me as we continue this exploration, delving deeper into the symphony that is reshaping the very fabric of our cultural landscape.

CHAPTER 2: THE MAESTRO'S TOOLKIT -

Crafting Harmony in the Fusion of AI and Music

In our journey through the intricate interplay of artificial intelligence (AI) and music, Chapter 2 unveils the fascinating realm of the Maestro's Toolkit. Imagine the conductor standing before a symphony, wielding a baton not only to guide musicians but to navigate the intricacies of algorithms and data. This chapter delves into the tools and technologies that compose the symphonic fabric of AI-infused music, exploring the maestro's arsenal and the symphony of possibilities it unlocks.

The Maestro's Baton: Understanding AI in Music Composition:

As we embark on this exploration, envision the maestro's baton as the AI algorithms that shape the essence of musical composition. These algorithms are the architects of melodies, harmonies, and rhythms, working tirelessly to decode the intricate language of music. Machine learning algorithms, a subset of AI, analyze vast datasets to discern patterns and structures inherent in diverse musical genres.

Imagine a conductor meticulously studying a musical score; AI algorithms scrutinize notations of musical compositions, learning the grammar and syntax of melodies. They become the maestro's baton, translating the intricate nuances of musical theory into a digital language that forms the foundation of AI-generated compositions.

Neural Networks: The Virtuoso's of Interpretation:

Enter the virtuoso's of interpretation—the neural networks. These are the bedrock of AI's cognitive prowess, akin to skilled instrumentalists interpreting the maestro's directives. Neural networks delve into the subtleties of musical expression, recognizing patterns and infusing compositions with emotion and depth.

Just as a seasoned cellist draws emotion from the strings, neural networks extract sentiment and tone from data. They learn not just the notes but the emotional resonance of music, adding a layer of sophistication to AI-generated compositions. This symbiotic relationship between algorithms and neural networks mirrors the interplay between a composer and a skilled orchestra.

The Crescendo of Generative Algorithms:

Generative algorithms emerge as key players in the maestro's toolkit, orchestrating a crescendo of creative possibilities. These algorithms possess the unique ability to autonomously produce music, generating compositions that defy traditional constraints. Imagine a composer collaborating with an invisible muse, one that suggests novel ideas and directions.

Generative algorithms analyze existing musical pieces, absorbing their essence to create something entirely new. They open doors to unexplored realms of creativity, pushing the boundaries of what we consider musically feasible. The symphony of generative algorithms unfolds as a dialogue between tradition and innovation, with each algorithmic iteration contributing to the evolving landscape of musical expression.

Human-AI Collaboration: The Harmonic Convergence:

In this chapter, we witness the harmonious convergence of human ingenuity and artificial intelligence. It's not a competition but a collaboration—a duet where human composers and AI algorithms create a synergy that transcends individual capabilities. Picture a composer seated at a grand piano, hands moving effortlessly over the keys while an AI system sits adjacent, contributing ideas and nuances in real-time.

Human-AI collaboration sparks a creative dialogue that stretches the boundaries of musical innovation. The maestro's toolkit becomes an extension of the composer's imagination, offering a repertoire of possibilities that would be unattainable through traditional means. Together, human and AI navigate the delicate balance between intuition and computation, weaving a tapestry of melodies that defy easy classification.

Real-world Orchestration: A Case Study in Harmony:

To ground our theoretical exploration, let's delve into a real-world case study that exemplifies the orchestration of AI and music. Google's Magenta project stands as a beacon in the realm of AI-driven creativity. Magenta is an open-source research project exploring the role of machine learning as a tool in the creative process, particularly in music and art.

Explore the symphony of Magenta through this link:
    Google Magenta
    https://magenta.tensorflow.org/

Magenta's toolkit includes neural network models capable of generating melodies, harmonies, and even entire musical compositions. It is a testament to the collaborative potential of AI, inviting musicians and artists to explore new frontiers in creativity. Magenta's open-source nature democratizes access to the maestro's toolkit, allowing a diverse array of creators to contribute to the ever-expanding repertoire of AI-generated music.

The Ethereal Dance of Algorithmic Improvisation:

Within the maestro's toolkit, algorithmic improvisation emerges as a captivating dance between structure and spontaneity. Imagine a jazz ensemble where musicians engage in improvisational dialogues, responding to each other's cues. In the realm of AI and music, algorithms engage in a similar dance, creating spontaneous variations that maintain coherence within the musical framework.

Algorithmic improvisation brings an element of unpredictability to AI-generated music. It is not mere repetition of learned patterns but an exploration of the unknown, a dance where algorithms take creative risks. This dynamic interplay between structure and spontaneity elevates the maestro's toolkit to a realm where the unexpected becomes an integral part of the creative process.

Sonic Aesthetics: Crafting Soundscapes with AI:

Our exploration extends beyond traditional notions of melody and harmony to delve into the sonic aesthetics crafted by AI. Picture a painter selecting colors to evoke emotions on a canvas; AI algorithms curate sonic palettes, determining the timbre, texture, and spatial dimensions of sound. This goes beyond the composition itself, influencing the very fabric of how music is perceived.

AI-generated soundscapes are not bound by the limitations of physical instruments. They can emulate traditional instruments, morphing seamlessly into electronic beats or transcending into avant-garde sonic territories. The maestro's toolkit empowers composers to explore a kaleidoscope of sonic possibilities, shaping not only what is heard but how it is experienced.

The Confluence of Ethical Considerations:

As our exploration of the maestro's toolkit unfolds, the symphony is underscored by the lingering notes of ethical considerations. The convergence of AI and music prompts us to reflect on questions of authorship, ownership, and cultural implications. How do we navigate a landscape where AI algorithms contribute to the creative process, challenging established norms?

The ethical considerations resonate like a quiet undertone,

reminding us of the responsibility that comes with wielding the maestro's toolkit. As we compose AI-infused music, we must consider the implications on the cultural landscape, respecting the rights of creators and acknowledging the potential impact on artistic traditions.

Conclusion: The Ongoing Symphony:

As we conclude this chapter, the maestro's toolkit stands as a testament to the transformative power of AI in the realm of music. It is a dynamic ensemble of algorithms, neural networks, generative processes, and collaborative endeavors that propels the art form into uncharted territories.

Our exploration of the maestro's toolkit unveils a symphony of possibilities, where the boundaries between human and artificial creativity blur. It beckons us to embrace a future where composers, armed with a digital arsenal, navigate the nuanced landscape of musical expression.

The ongoing symphony promises new movements, unexplored harmonies, and the continued evolution of a musical language shaped by the intricate interplay of human passion and artificial intelligence.

CHAPTER 3: THE ART OF INSPIRATION -

A Symphony of Creativity in the Intersection of AI and Music

In our continuing exploration of the intricate interweaving of artificial intelligence (AI) and music, Chapter 3 invites us to delve into "The Art of Inspiration." This chapter is a deep dive into the transformative power of AI as a muse, a collaborator, and a catalyst for new dimensions of creativity within the realm of music. As we navigate this chapter, envision a canvas where the strokes of AI influence not only the composition process but also the very essence of artistic inspiration.

The Evolving Creative Landscape:

The Art of Inspiration opens with a panorama of the evolving creative landscape shaped by the integration of AI and music. Imagine standing at the threshold of a vast expanse where traditional notions of inspiration are infused with the algorithms and data-driven insights of artificial intelligence. This fusion challenges preconceived ideas about the genesis of creative ideas, redefining the role of inspiration in the musical journey.

AI, as a creative collaborator, expands the palette from which artists draw inspiration. Instead of a solitary muse, artists engage in a dynamic dialogue with algorithms, exploring uncharted territories of sound, structure, and emotion. The landscape of inspiration broadens, becoming a rich tapestry woven with the threads of human intuition and machine-driven insights.

The Symphony of Data:

At the heart of AI's role in inspiring musical creation lies the symphony of data. Consider the vastness of musical datasets containing centuries of compositions, genres, and cultural nuances. These datasets become a treasure trove from which AI extracts patterns, styles, and trends, acting as a reservoir of inspiration for composers.

Imagine a composer standing before a vast library, not of sheet music, but of data points representing the collective history of music. AI algorithms act as virtuoso librarians, sifting through this vast repository to offer snippets of inspiration, suggesting novel chord progressions, melodic structures, or rhythmic variations. The symphony of data becomes a source of endless inspiration, enabling artists to draw from the wisdom of musical history while pushing the boundaries of contemporary expression.

Innovation Through Collaboration:

One of the defining characteristics of the AI-infused creative process is the spirit of collaboration. Artists collaborate not only with their human peers but also with AI systems that bring a unique perspective to the table. Envision a studio where a composer sits across from an AI algorithm, engaged in a collaborative exchange of ideas, each influencing the other in a harmonious dance of creativity.

AI, as a collaborator, introduces fresh perspectives and challenges the status quo. It is not a passive tool but an active participant in the creative dialogue. The result is a fusion of human artistry and machine intelligence, a collaborative masterpiece that transcends the limitations of individual creativity. This collaborative spirit redefines the artist's relationship with inspiration, turning it into a dynamic exchange that sparks innovation.

The Emotional Palette:

One of the remarkable aspects of AI's contribution to musical inspiration is its ability to navigate the emotional landscape of music. Picture an artist selecting colors from a palette to evoke specific emotions in a painting. AI algorithms similarly curate an emotional palette, offering suggestions for musical elements that resonate with specific moods, feelings, or atmospheres.

Through sentiment analysis and emotional mapping, AI systems can discern the emotional undercurrents of diverse musical compositions. This capability transforms the creative process, allowing artists to explore and amplify emotional dimensions within their work. The result is a symphony that not only sounds captivating but also resonates on a deep emotional level, creating a profound connection with the listener.

Case Study: AI-Driven Emotional Resonance in Music:

To illustrate the impact of AI on emotional resonance in music, let's turn our attention to a notable case study: IBM's Watson Beat. Watson Beat is an AI system developed by IBM that uses machine learning algorithms to analyze musical data and generate compositions. Its unique feature lies in its ability to create music that emotionally resonates with the listener.

Explore the emotional resonance of Watson Beat through this link:
> IBM Watson Beat
> https://www.ibm.com/cloud/watson-beat

Watson Beat's algorithms analyze not only the structural elements of music but also the emotional content. By understanding the emotional impact of different musical components, the system generates compositions that evoke specific feelings. This case study exemplifies the potential of AI to enhance the emotional depth of music, offering a glimpse into the future where artists leverage AI to craft emotionally compelling sonic experiences.

The Empowerment of Creativity:

As we navigate The Art of Inspiration, it becomes evident that AI serves as an empowering force for creativity. Imagine an artist equipped with an augmented palette of inspiration, drawn not only from personal experiences but also from the collective intelligence embedded in AI algorithms. This empowerment transcends traditional notions of artistic isolation, fostering a collaborative environment where artists feel emboldened to explore new territories.

AI's ability to inspire creativity lies not only in its analytical capabilities but also in its capacity to break down creative barriers. It encourages risk-taking and experimentation, offering a safety net that allows artists to push the boundaries of their craft. The result is a renaissance of creativity where inspiration flows freely, guided by the dynamic interplay between human ingenuity and artificial intelligence.

The Emergence of Genre-Bending:

In the landscape of AI-driven inspiration, traditional genre boundaries become fluid, paving the way for the emergence of genre-bending musical expressions. Envision a spectrum where classical orchestration seamlessly merges with electronic beats, or where jazz improvisation converges with algorithmically generated structures. AI's influence transcends genre limitations, encouraging artists to explore hybrid forms that defy easy categorization.

The boundaries between genres blur as AI algorithms draw inspiration from diverse musical traditions, creating compositions that weave together threads of influence. This genre-bending phenomenon transforms the musical landscape, offering listeners a rich and eclectic tapestry of sounds that challenge preconceived notions of musical identity.

Ethical Considerations: Navigating the Intersection of Creativity and Control:

In the midst of this symphony of inspiration, it is crucial to navigate the ethical considerations that arise at the intersection of creativity and control. As artists embrace AI as a muse, questions of authorship, ownership, and creative autonomy come to the forefront. How do we strike a balance between the guidance AI provides and the individual expression of the artist?

The relationship between artist and AI demands careful consideration of ethical frameworks. Artists must be conscious of the potential impact on cultural heritage, intellectual property, and the democratization of creative tools. The exploration of AI-driven inspiration necessitates a thoughtful approach that safeguards the integrity of artistic expression while embracing the transformative potential of technology.

Conclusion: A Symphony Unfolding:

As we bring The Art of Inspiration to a crescendo, we stand at the threshold of a symphony unfolding—a harmonious collaboration between human creativity and artificial intelligence. The art of inspiration is no longer confined to the musings of a solitary mind; it resonates in the collective intelligence of algorithms and the boundless possibilities they bring.

In this chapter, we've explored the evolving creative landscape, the symphony of data, the collaborative spirit, the emotional palette, and the empowerment of creativity facilitated by AI. We've witnessed genre boundaries dissolve, giving rise to a musical renaissance where inspiration knows no limits.

As we transition to the next movement of our exploration, envision a future where artists, empowered by AI-driven inspiration, continue to push the boundaries of musical expression. The symphony of creativity is in a perpetual state of evolution, and the intersection of AI and music propels us into uncharted realms of artistic possibility.

CHAPTER 4: CRAFTING THE MELODY -

The Intricate Dance of AI and Musical Expression

As our exploration of the intricate world where artificial intelligence (AI) is woven with music continues, Chapter 4 takes center stage, immersing us in the delicate art of crafting the melody. Picture a blank musical canvas awaiting the strokes of both human intuition and machine-driven algorithms. This chapter unravels the nuanced dance between human composers and AI systems as they collaboratively shape the very heart of music—the melody.

The Essence of Melody:

At the heart of every musical composition lies the melody—a sequence of notes that captures the essence of emotion, narrative, and expression. As we venture into Crafting the Melody, envision the melody as the soulful core of a musical piece, a thread that weaves through the fabric of sound to convey the artist's intentions. In the collaboration between humans and AI, crafting the melody becomes a symbiotic dance, where the strengths of each partner contribute to the harmonious whole.

AI as a Creative Catalyst:

AI, in the realm of music, assumes the role of a creative catalyst, a force that propels the artistic process forward. Imagine an artist standing before a canvas, palette in hand, with an AI system acting as an intuitive guide, suggesting colors and brushstrokes. Similarly, in the crafting of melodies, AI serves as a collaborator, offering suggestions, generating ideas, and inspiring new musical directions.

The creative catalyst aspect of AI is particularly pronounced in the realm of melody. Algorithms, infused with the knowledge of diverse musical genres, historical compositions, and contemporary trends, become sources of inspiration for human composers. They are not mere tools but virtual companions, contributing to the compositional journey in ways that challenge and complement human intuition.

AI-Driven Melodic Exploration:

Crafting the melody with AI involves a process of exploration that transcends traditional compositional boundaries. Imagine a composer embarking on a musical journey with an AI system, venturing into uncharted territories where conventional norms are questioned, and innovation takes center stage.

AI-driven melodic exploration begins with the analysis of vast musical datasets, encompassing everything from classical symphonies to avant-garde electronic compositions. This exploration is not limited by genre, era, or cultural context. It involves algorithms discerning patterns, identifying melodic arcs, and distilling the essence of diverse musical expressions. The result is a rich reservoir of melodic possibilities, waiting to be discovered by the guiding hands of composers.

Generative Algorithms and Melodic Creativity:

At the core of crafting the melody with AI are generative algorithms, the virtuoso's of spontaneous creation. These algorithms are programmed to autonomously generate melodic sequences, offering a fusion of structure and unpredictability. Imagine a composer collaborating with an algorithmic muse, where each iteration of the algorithm yields a unique melodic variation.

Generative algorithms analyze the intricacies of melodic patterns, learning not only from existing compositions but also from the stylistic preferences of the collaborating composer. The dance between the composer's vision and the algorithm's generative capacity results in a dynamic interplay that challenges the boundaries of traditional melodic composition. The generated melodies may surprise, inspire, or provide a starting point for further refinement, becoming a source of continuous creative exploration.

Human-AI Co-Creation: The Composer's Duet:

In the intricate dance of crafting the melody, human-AI co-creation emerges as a pivotal theme. This is not a solo performance by either the composer or the AI system but a duet —a collaborative dialogue where ideas are exchanged, refined, and woven into the melodic tapestry.

Picture a composer seated at a piano, engaging in a musical conversation with an AI system. The AI system, equipped with a vast array of melodic possibilities, responds to the composer's cues, suggesting variations, harmonies, or rhythmic shifts. The composer, in turn, interprets and refines these suggestions, injecting a unique human touch that resonates with emotion and intent.

The composer's duet with AI is a dance of interpretation and guidance. It involves moments of improvisation where the AI system suggests melodic pathways, and the composer, drawing from personal intuition, refines and shapes these suggestions. This dynamic collaboration challenges the notion of the solitary genius, embracing a model of co-creation that leverages the strengths of both human and artificial intelligence.

Real-world Synthesis: A Case Study in Melodic Collaboration:

To illustrate the real-world synthesis of human-AI co-creation in crafting melodies, let's delve into a case study: AIVA (Artificial Intelligence Virtual Artist). AIVA is an AI system developed by the company AIVA Labs, designed to compose classical music autonomously.

Explore the melodic creations of AIVA through this link:
AIVA
https://www.aiva.ai/

AIVA serves as an example of how AI can be an active collaborator in the creative process. Composers working with AIVA have described the experience as a symbiotic relationship, where the AI system generates musical ideas, and the composers provide the artistic direction and emotional nuance. This case study exemplifies how AI-driven melodic collaboration can result in compositions that blend the best of human and machine creativity.

Emotional Resonance in Melody:

Crafting the melody involves not only the technical aspects of note selection and arrangement but also the emotional resonance embedded in the music. AI systems, equipped with the ability to analyze emotional content in music, contribute to the crafting of melodies that evoke specific feelings, moods, or atmospheres.

Imagine an AI system discerning the emotional nuances within a melodic sequence, understanding how certain note combinations or rhythmic patterns resonate with joy, melancholy, tension, or serenity. This emotional intelligence becomes a guiding force, influencing the composer's decisions in crafting melodies that convey a desired emotional impact.

The fusion of emotional resonance and melodic creativity is a testament to the evolving capabilities of AI in understanding and interpreting the complex language of human emotion through music. It opens avenues for composers to explore nuanced emotional landscapes, enhancing the expressive depth of their melodic compositions.

Sonic Innovation: The Intersection of Melody and Sound Design:

In the intricate world of AI and music, the crafting of melody is inseparable from the broader realm of sonic innovation. Envision a composer not only selecting individual notes but also manipulating the very fabric of sound—its timbre, texture, and spatial dimensions. AI contributes to this sonic innovation by offering new possibilities in sound design that enrich the melodic experience.

Consider an AI system capable of analyzing the sonic characteristics of various instruments and genres. This analysis allows composers to experiment with novel combinations, pushing beyond the constraints of traditional instrumentation. The result is a fusion of melodic creativity and sonic exploration, where AI algorithms contribute to the creation of unique, sonically rich melodies that defy conventional norms.

Ethical Considerations: Navigating Authorship and Originality:

As we navigate the intricate dance of crafting the melody with AI, ethical considerations surrounding authorship and originality come to the forefront. The collaborative nature of human-AI co-creation prompts reflection on questions of artistic ownership and the definition of what constitutes an original composition.

Artists and technologists alike must navigate the ethical landscape, considering issues such as intellectual property rights, proper attribution, and the potential impact on the recognition of individual creative contributions. Striking a balance between leveraging AI as a tool for inspiration and maintaining the integrity of artistic authorship becomes a critical aspect of the melodic crafting process.

The Future Harmonies: A Glimpse Ahead:

As Crafting the Melody draws to a close, we stand at the threshold of the future harmonies that await in the ever-evolving landscape of AI and music. The dance between human creativity and artificial intelligence in crafting melodies is a dynamic, ongoing symphony—one that promises to unfold new dimensions of expression, innovation, and emotional resonance.

The journey of crafting melodies with AI is not a destination but a continuous exploration, an evolving narrative where composers and AI systems engage in a perpetual dialogue. As we transition to the next chapter of our exploration, envision a future where the melodies crafted through this collaborative dance resonate with beauty, complexity, and the shared language of human and artificial creativity.

CHAPTER 5:
HARMONIC ALCHEMY -

The Fusion of AI and Music in Creating Sonic Masterpieces

As we delve deeper into the intricate world where artificial intelligence (AI) is interwoven with music, Chapter 5 takes us on a mesmerizing journey into the realm of Harmonic Alchemy. Imagine a workshop where algorithms, creativity, and innovation coalesce to transmute musical elements into sonic masterpieces. In this chapter, we explore the transformative power of AI in harmonizing diverse musical components, creating compositions that resonate with depth, complexity, and an otherworldly beauty.

The Alchemy of Harmonic Fusion:

Harmonic Alchemy is the art of blending disparate musical elements into a cohesive whole, transcending the sum of its parts. Picture an alchemist's laboratory where AI algorithms serve as the mystical catalysts, fusing melodies, rhythms, and harmonies to birth compositions that defy traditional classification. The metaphorical crucible of Harmonic Alchemy represents the transformative process through which AI elevates musical creation to unprecedented heights.

In this alchemical workshop, the boundaries between genres blur, and the distinctions between acoustic and electronic instruments become fluid. AI acts as the alchemist's apprentice, learning from the rich history of music, understanding the intricacies of various styles, and contributing to the creation of harmonies that resonate with both familiarity and innovation.

AI as a Harmonic Composer:

At the heart of Harmonic Alchemy lies the concept of AI as a harmonic composer—an entity capable of crafting intricate musical structures that marry diverse elements seamlessly. Envision an AI system not only analyzing existing compositions but also composing entirely new harmonic progressions, chord structures, and rhythmic patterns. This harmonic composer is not bound by convention but explores the uncharted territories of sound, guided by the collaborative hand of human composers.

The harmonies generated by AI often push beyond traditional tonal boundaries, introducing novel combinations that challenge preconceived notions of musical structure. This innovation expands the sonic palette, enriching compositions with harmonic complexities that captivate the listener's ear. The harmonic composer becomes a partner in the creative process, contributing to the evolution of musical expression.

Generative Algorithms and Harmonic Complexity:

Generative algorithms, the maestros of spontaneity, play a pivotal role in the harmonic complexity achieved through AI. These algorithms, trained on vast datasets and immersed in the nuances of musical theory, have the ability to generate intricate harmonic sequences that may elude traditional composition methods. Imagine an algorithmic virtuoso weaving together chords, progressions, and counterpoint, creating harmonic tapestries that defy easy categorization.

The harmonies produced by generative algorithms reflect a fusion of learned patterns and novel interpretations. The algorithms draw inspiration from the entirety of musical history, distilling complex harmonic relationships from diverse genres and traditions. The result is a harmonic richness that extends beyond the predictable, inviting listeners into a sonic landscape where surprise and innovation harmonize in harmonious unity.

Human-AI Harmonic Collaboration: A Symphony in Partnership:

The collaborative symphony between human composers and AI in Harmonic Alchemy is akin to a dance of partnership, where each participant contributes unique strengths to the creation of harmonic masterpieces. Picture a composer sitting at the piano, exchanging ideas with an AI system that suggests harmonic progressions, tonal shifts, and modulations. The dialogue is not a mere exchange but a harmonious partnership that transcends individual capabilities.

Human-AI harmonic collaboration involves a fluid exchange of musical ideas, with the AI system functioning as a harmonic guide and co-creator. The composer interprets the suggestions, infusing them with personal expression, emotion, and artistic intent. This dynamic partnership allows for the exploration of harmonic territories that may not have been conceivable through traditional methods alone.

Consider an AI system suggesting a modulation to an unexpected key during a composition. The composer, informed by both intuition and the AI's harmonic knowledge, evaluates the suggestion and decides whether to embrace or adapt it. This collaborative decision-making process becomes a hallmark of Harmonic Alchemy, where the sumptuous harmonies emerge from the synergy of human and artificial creativity.

Real-world Synthesis: A Case Study in Harmonic Innovation:

To illustrate the real-world synthesis of Harmonic Alchemy, let's explore a case study: Google's Magenta Studio. Magenta Studio is an open-source project that leverages machine learning to explore new ways of making music and art.

Explore the harmonic innovations of Magenta Studio through this link:
Google Magenta Studio

https://magenta.tensorflow.org/studio

Magenta Studio offers tools that allow musicians and composers to experiment with harmonies and explore new sonic territories. The project exemplifies how AI can be a valuable companion in the creative process, suggesting harmonic possibilities and facilitating harmonic innovation. It serves as a testament to the collaborative potential of Harmonic Alchemy in the realm of music.

Sonic Textures: The Alchemical Marriage of Harmonies and Timbres:

In Harmonic Alchemy, the exploration of sonic textures becomes an integral facet of the creative process. Envision a painter meticulously blending colors on a canvas to achieve a desired texture. Similarly, composers and AI engage in an alchemical marriage of harmonies and timbres, crafting sonic textures that elevate the listening experience.

AI contributes to this sonic alchemy by offering insights into innovative timbral combinations. Through the analysis of vast musical datasets, AI systems discern the sonic characteristics of different instruments and genres. This knowledge empowers composers to experiment with unconventional pairings, creating harmonic textures that not only convey emotion but also evoke a visceral response from the audience.

Consider an AI system suggesting a fusion of orchestral strings with electronic synthesizers, resulting in a harmonic tapestry that marries the warmth of classical instrumentation with the cutting-edge timbres of electronic elements. This exploration of sonic textures transforms Harmonic Alchemy into a multisensory experience, where the fusion of harmonies and timbres captivates the imagination.

The Ethereal Dance of Modulation:

Modulation, the ethereal dance of harmonic transition between different keys, holds a special place in Harmonic Alchemy. Imagine a composition seamlessly shifting from one key to another, guided by the invisible hand of AI algorithms. Modulation becomes a tool for harmonic exploration, allowing composers to traverse tonal landscapes with fluidity and grace.

AI algorithms analyze the harmonic structures of diverse musical compositions, learning the art of modulation from classical traditions to contemporary innovations. This knowledge empowers AI to suggest modulations that enhance the emotional arc of a composition, creating harmonic journeys that surprise and captivate the listener.

The dance of modulation in Harmonic Alchemy is not limited to traditional tonalities. AI introduces the possibility of exploring microtonal modulations, where the harmonic landscape extends beyond the constraints of standard Western scales. This avant-garde approach to modulation challenges conventional harmonic expectations, offering a fresh perspective on how music can evolve through AI-driven innovation.

The Algorithmic Conductor: Directing Harmonic Symphonies:

In the orchestration of Harmonic Alchemy, envision the presence of an algorithmic conductor—a virtual maestro capable of directing harmonic symphonies with precision and flair. This conductor is not bound by the limitations of a physical baton but wields the power of algorithms to shape and guide harmonic progressions.

The algorithmic conductor, informed by the collective knowledge of musical theory and harmonic conventions, becomes an invaluable guide for composers. It suggests harmonic resolutions, guides the exploration of tension and release, and orchestrates the harmonic dynamics of a composition. The result is a collaborative effort where the human composer interprets and refines the suggestions of the algorithmic conductor, leading to harmonic symphonies that resonate with complexity and cohesion.

Ethical Considerations: Navigating Harmonic Originality and Attribution:

As we immerse ourselves in Harmonic Alchemy, ethical considerations regarding harmonic originality and attribution come to the forefront. The collaborative nature of human-AI composition prompts reflection on questions of authorship, acknowledging the unique contributions of both human composers and AI algorithms to the harmonic landscape.

Artists and technologists must navigate the ethical complexities surrounding harmonic innovation, ensuring transparent attribution and recognition of the collaborative nature of the creative process. The alchemical fusion of harmonies demands a thoughtful approach to crediting both human and artificial contributors, acknowledging their respective roles in the creation of sonic masterpieces.

Conclusion: The Harmonic Resonance Continues:

As Harmonic Alchemy concludes its symphony, we find ourselves standing at the precipice of a musical landscape transformed by the interplay of AI and human creativity. The alchemical fusion of harmonies, melodies, and textures has given rise to sonic masterpieces that challenge conventions, inspire emotion, and beckon listeners into unexplored realms.

The journey of Harmonic Alchemy is ongoing, with the promise of continued innovation and exploration in the intricate world where AI is woven with music. As we transition to the next chapter of our exploration, envision a future where Harmonic Alchemy continues to shape the sonic landscape, inviting composers and listeners alike to immerse themselves in the ever-evolving symphony of artificial and human creativity.

CHAPTER 6: RHYTHMIC WIZARDRY -

Unveiling the Enchantment of AI in the Tapestry of Music

In our continuing exploration of the intricate world where artificial intelligence (AI) is woven with music, Chapter 6 invites us to unravel the mysteries of "Rhythmic Wizardry." Picture a realm where algorithms, like magical incantations, breathe life into rhythmic patterns, transforming beats into a mesmerizing dance of sound. This chapter delves into the enchantment of AI in shaping rhythm, exploring how algorithms contribute to the rhythmic tapestry of music, creating compositions that defy the constraints of traditional time signatures.

The Essence of Rhythm:

Rhythm is the heartbeat of music, the invisible force that propels compositions forward and captivates listeners with its pulse. As we delve into Rhythmic Wizardry, envision rhythm not just as a sequence of beats but as a dynamic, ever-shifting landscape where AI serves as a wizard, conjuring patterns that elevate the very essence of musical time.

In this exploration, rhythm becomes a canvas for artistic expression, and AI emerges as the wizard who weaves intricate patterns, guides tempos, and introduces a sense of unpredictability into the rhythmic journey. The essence of rhythm, in the world of AI-infused music, transcends the boundaries of tradition, inviting composers and listeners into a realm of enchantment.

AI as the Rhythmic Conjurer:

At the heart of Rhythmic Wizardry lies the concept of AI as the rhythmic conjurer—a creative force capable of summoning rhythmic patterns that push the boundaries of convention. Envision an algorithmic sorcerer, well-versed in the language of diverse musical genres and rhythmic traditions, shaping the very fabric of time in collaboration with human composers.

The rhythmic conjurer, informed by vast datasets of rhythmic variations, becomes a source of inspiration for artists seeking to break free from rhythmic norms. This AI-driven creativity is not about adhering to a fixed grid but about exploring the vast expanse of rhythmic possibilities, introducing subtle nuances and unexpected twists that captivate the listener's ear.

Generative Algorithms and Rhythmic Exploration:

Generative algorithms, the virtuoso's of spontaneity, play a pivotal role in the rhythmic exploration facilitated by AI. These algorithms analyze diverse rhythmic patterns, from traditional beats to avant-garde percussive expressions, and autonomously generate rhythmic sequences that transcend conventional expectations.

Imagine a drummer collaborating with an algorithmic partner, where each beat and accent is a product of this dynamic interchange. The generative nature of these algorithms allows for rhythmic variations that extend beyond the limitations of pre-programmed patterns. This rhythmic exploration challenges composers to break away from familiar cadences, introducing a sense of unpredictability that enriches the overall listening experience.

Human-AI Rhythmic Collaboration: The Dance of Co-Creation:

The dance of co-creation between human composers and AI in Rhythmic Wizardry is akin to a rhythmic dialogue, where each partner contributes unique elements to the dance. Picture a percussionist engaging in a rhythmic conversation with an AI system, where suggestions and responses flow seamlessly, creating a rhythmic tapestry that marries the precision of algorithms with the human touch.

Human-AI rhythmic collaboration involves a dynamic exchange of ideas, with the AI system suggesting variations, polyrhythms, and percussive accents. The human composer, in turn, interprets and refines these suggestions, infusing the rhythms with emotion, intention, and artistic flair. The resulting composition becomes a testament to the synergy between human intuition and algorithmic precision.

Consider a scenario where an AI system suggests a polyrhythmic interplay between different percussive elements. The human composer, drawing from personal experience and musical sensibility, decides how to weave these rhythmic elements into the composition. This collaborative dance embraces the strengths of both human and artificial creativity, creating rhythmic expressions that transcend the limitations of singular authorship.

Real-world Synthesis: A Case Study in Rhythmic Innovation:

To illustrate the real-world synthesis of Rhythmic Wizardry, let's explore a case study: Sony's Flow Machines. Flow Machines is an AI system designed to assist composers in creating music with an emphasis on rhythm and melodic structures.

Explore the rhythmic innovations of Flow Machines through this link:
Sony Flow Machines
https://www.flow-machines.com/

Flow Machines employs generative algorithms to analyze vast

datasets of music, extracting rhythmic and melodic patterns. Composers using Flow Machines can then collaborate with the AI system to explore new rhythmic territories and create compositions that push the boundaries of traditional conventions. This case study exemplifies how AI serves as a rhythmic collaborator, enriching the creative process with innovative patterns and structures.

Polyrhythmic Possibilities: Expanding the Rhythmic Vocabulary:

In the enchanting realm of Rhythmic Wizardry, AI introduces the concept of polyrhythmic possibilities—a rhythmic vocabulary that extends beyond the constraints of a single time signature. Imagine a composition where different instruments or sections follow distinct rhythmic cycles, creating a layered and complex sonic experience.

Polyrhythmic exploration involves AI algorithms analyzing the rhythmic characteristics of diverse musical genres, from Afro-Cuban drumming to Indian classical rhythms. The algorithms learn the intricacies of polyrhythmic interactions and suggest combinations that add depth and complexity to compositions. This expansion of the rhythmic vocabulary invites artists to explore unconventional rhythmic relationships, resulting in compositions that resonate with a heightened sense of dynamism.

Consider a scenario where an AI system suggests the incorporation of a 5/4 time signature for a particular section of a composition while another instrument adheres to a traditional 4/4 time signature. The resulting polyrhythmic interplay creates a captivating tension and release, transforming the rhythmic landscape into a dynamic and ever-evolving tapestry.

Tempo Modulation: The Art of Rhythmic Flux:

In Rhythmic Wizardry, the art of tempo modulation becomes a spellbinding technique for composers and AI alike. Imagine a composition where the tempo seamlessly shifts, creating a sense of rhythmic flux that propels the listener through different emotional landscapes.

AI algorithms, with their understanding of diverse musical genres and historical compositions, contribute to the art of tempo modulation. The algorithms analyze the rhythmic patterns associated with changes in tempo, learning how different genres use variations in speed to convey mood and intensity. This knowledge empowers composers to experiment with tempo modulation as a narrative device, guiding the listener through rhythmic twists and turns.

The dance of tempo modulation is not confined to abrupt changes but can involve gradual shifts, creating a sense of gradual acceleration or deceleration. This dynamic rhythmic flux, guided by the collaborative interplay between human intuition and AI precision, adds a layer of sophistication to compositions, turning each transition in tempo into a rhythmic enchantment.

AI as the Drummer's Companion: Rhythmic Augmentation and Variation:

For drummers, AI serves as a companion in the exploration of rhythmic augmentation and variation. Envision a drummer engaging in a rhythmic conversation with an AI system, where suggestions for embellishments, fills, and variations are exchanged in real-time.

AI algorithms, trained on a vast array of drumming styles and techniques, offer drummers insights into rhythmic embellishments that go beyond traditional paradigms. The system can suggest variations in drum patterns, dynamic shifts, and intricate fills, elevating the rhythmic complexity of compositions.

Consider a drummer receiving real-time suggestions from an AI system during a live performance. The AI, attuned to the nuances of the ongoing musical context, offers rhythmic variations that complement the improvisational nature of the performance. This collaborative exchange transforms the drummer-AI relationship into a rhythmic partnership, expanding the drummer's expressive toolkit and contributing to the overall sonic experience.

Ethical Considerations: Navigating Rhythmic Authenticity and Cultural Sensitivity:

As we immerse ourselves in the enchantment of Rhythmic Wizardry, ethical considerations surrounding rhythmic authenticity and cultural sensitivity come to the forefront. AI algorithms, trained on diverse musical traditions, must navigate the delicate balance between innovation and cultural respect.

Composers and AI developers must be mindful of the cultural origins and contexts of rhythmic patterns suggested by AI systems. The exploration of rhythmic possibilities should be approached with an understanding of the cultural significance of different rhythmic traditions, ensuring that AI-driven compositions respect and honor the diversity of musical heritage.

Conclusion: The Rhythmic Spell Endures:

As Rhythmic Wizardry concludes its magical symphony, we find ourselves immersed in a world where AI and human creativity dance together in rhythmic harmony. The rhythmic enchantment created by algorithms adds layers of complexity, unpredictability, and innovation to the musical landscape.

The journey of Rhythmic Wizardry is ongoing, with the promise of continued exploration and discovery in the intricate world where AI is woven with music. As we transition to the next chapter of our exploration, envision a future where rhythmic wizardry continues to captivate, inspire, and push the boundaries of what is musically possible.

CHAPTER 7: INSTRUMENTATION SYMPHONY -

The Harmonious Collaboration of AI and Musical Instruments

In our continuing odyssey through the intricate world where artificial intelligence (AI) is interwoven with music, Chapter 7 invites us into the enchanting realm of "Instrumentation Symphony." Imagine a symphony where algorithms harmonize with traditional and electronic instruments, creating compositions that push the boundaries of sonic possibility. This chapter delves into the collaborative tapestry of AI and musical instruments, exploring how algorithms and performers join forces to redefine the landscape of musical instrumentation.

The Essence of Instrumentation:

Instrumentation is the art of selecting and orchestrating instruments to bring a musical composition to life. In Instrumentation Symphony, this art form is elevated to new heights as AI algorithms become active participants in the orchestral arrangement. Picture a conductor collaborating with lines of code, shaping the interplay of instruments, textures, and timbres to craft a symphony that transcends traditional boundaries.

In this exploration, instrumentation is not a static choice but a dynamic process where AI contributes to the decision-making, offering insights into novel instrument combinations, tonal possibilities, and sonic textures. The essence of instrumentation, in the world of AI-infused music, lies in the harmonious marriage of tradition and innovation.

AI as the Orchestrator:

At the heart of Instrumentation Symphony lies the concept of AI as the orchestrator—a creative force guiding the selection, arrangement, and interaction of musical instruments. Envision an algorithmic conductor leading an orchestra of both traditional and virtual instruments, translating data into melodies, harmonies, and timbral expressions.

The orchestrator AI analyzes vast datasets encompassing the sonic profiles of diverse instruments and genres. This knowledge allows the algorithm to suggest instrument combinations that may not have been conventionally explored. The role of the orchestrator extends beyond recommending instruments; it involves shaping the dynamic relationships between them, orchestrating transitions, and fostering a collaborative interplay between human performers and virtual instruments.

Generative Algorithms and Sonic Exploration:

Generative algorithms, the wizards of spontaneous creation, play a pivotal role in the sonic exploration facilitated by AI in Instrumentation Symphony. These algorithms are not confined to generating melodies or harmonies but extend their creativity to crafting sonic textures, timbral nuances, and expressive phrasing.

Imagine an algorithmic maestro suggesting the integration of an electronic synthesizer with a classical string section, creating a fusion that transcends traditional instrumentation. The generative nature of these algorithms allows for the exploration of sonic territories that push the boundaries of conventional orchestration. The result is a sonic palette enriched with unexpected timbral combinations and textural diversity.

Human-AI Instrumental Collaboration: A Symphony in Unity:

The collaborative symphony between human instrumentalists and AI in Instrumentation Symphony is a testament to the unity of traditional artistry and technological innovation. Picture a violinist collaborating with an AI orchestrator, where each note played is part of a larger symphony that transcends the capabilities of any individual musician.

Human-AI instrumental collaboration involves a dynamic exchange of ideas. The AI orchestrator suggests instrument pairings, articulations, and expressive techniques based on its analysis of musical data. The human instrumentalist, drawing from years of training and interpretive skill, infuses these suggestions with emotion, nuance, and personal expression.

Consider a scenario where an AI suggests a brass section complementing a solo cello, enhancing the emotive power of a musical passage. The cellist, informed by the AI's suggestion, adapts the performance to harmonize with the suggested brass accompaniment. This dynamic collaboration creates a symphony in which the boundaries between human and artificial contributions blur, resulting in a unified and harmonious musical expression.

Real-world Synthesis: A Case Study in Instrumental Fusion:

To illustrate the real-world synthesis of Instrumentation Symphony, let's explore a case study: IBM's Watson Beat. Watson Beat is an AI system designed to generate musical compositions by analyzing various musical elements, including instrumentation, and providing creative suggestions.

Explore the instrumental fusion possibilities of Watson Beat through this link:
> IBM Watson Beat
> https://www.ibm.com/cloud/watson-beat

Once again, Watson Beat allows composers and musicians to experiment with different instrumentation and genres, offering suggestions based on its analysis of vast musical datasets. This case study exemplifies how AI can serve as a collaborator in the creative process, contributing to the exploration of novel instrument combinations and expanding the sonic palette of musical compositions.

Timbral Innovation: The Intersection of Instruments and Sonic Textures:

In the intricate world of AI and music, Instrumentation Symphony goes beyond traditional instrument choices, embracing timbral innovation as a key element of sonic exploration. Envision a composer not only selecting instruments but also shaping the very fabric of sound—the timbre, texture, and sonic qualities of each instrument.

AI contributes to timbral innovation by offering insights into unconventional instrument pairings and sonic textures. The algorithms analyze the sonic characteristics of various instruments, learning how different timbres interact and complement each other. This knowledge empowers composers to experiment with novel combinations, creating instrumental textures that defy conventional norms.

Consider an AI suggesting the incorporation of a synthesizer with a traditional flute, exploring how the electronic and acoustic timbres can merge to create a unique sonic landscape. This intersection of instruments and sonic textures transforms Instrumentation Symphony into a multisensory experience, where timbral innovation becomes a driving force in shaping the musical narrative.

Expressive Orchestration: Conveying Emotion through Instrumentation:

In the realm of Instrumentation Symphony, the selection and orchestration of instruments become vehicles for conveying emotion. Envision an AI orchestrator discerning the emotional nuances within a composition and suggesting instrument combinations that enhance the intended mood, atmosphere, or narrative.

AI algorithms, equipped with the ability to analyze emotional content in music, contribute to the expressive orchestration by recommending instruments that resonate with specific feelings. Imagine a composition where a melancholic cello solo is complemented by the ethereal tones of a synthesized choir, creating a poignant and evocative musical moment.

The expressive orchestration facilitated by AI transcends the technical aspects of instrumentation. It involves understanding how different instruments convey emotion, and how their combinations can evoke a range of feelings. This nuanced approach to instrumentation enriches the emotional depth of compositions, allowing composers to communicate with listeners on a profound and visceral level.

AI as the Composer's Assistant: Facilitating Instrumental Experimentation:

In the collaborative process of Instrumentation Symphony, AI assumes the role of the composer's assistant, offering valuable insights and facilitating instrumental experimentation. Imagine a composer exploring a new composition, experimenting with different instrumentation's and arrangements to find the perfect sonic palette.

AI algorithms, trained on diverse musical genres and historical compositions, serve as assistants that suggest instrument combinations, dynamic contrasts, and timbral variations. The composer can interact with these suggestions in real-time, adjusting and refining the instrumentation to suit their artistic vision. This collaborative exchange between the composer and AI transforms the creative process into a dynamic exploration, where the composer's intuition is complemented by the algorithm's analytical prowess.

Consider a composer using an AI assistant to experiment with the instrumentation of a symphonic piece. The AI suggests incorporating unconventional instruments, such as electronic synthesizers or ethnic percussion, to add a contemporary flair. The composer, inspired by these suggestions, refines the orchestration to create a composition that blends tradition and innovation seamlessly.

Ethical Considerations: Navigating Originality and Cultural Sensitivity:

As we navigate the symphonic landscape of Instrumentation Symphony, ethical considerations surrounding originality and cultural sensitivity come to the forefront. AI algorithms, while offering creative suggestions, must navigate the delicate balance between innovation and respect for musical traditions.

Composers and AI developers must be mindful of the cultural origins of different instruments and musical styles. The exploration of novel instrument combinations should be approached with an understanding of the cultural significance of each instrument. Additionally, considerations of originality and proper attribution become crucial in acknowledging the collaborative nature of AI-driven instrumental compositions.

Conclusion: The Symphony Resounds:

As Instrumentation Symphony concludes its orchestral journey, we find ourselves immersed in a world where AI and human creativity converge in harmonious collaboration. The symphony of instruments, guided by algorithms and human intuition, transcends the boundaries of traditional orchestration, giving rise to compositions that captivate the imagination.

The journey of Instrumentation Symphony is ongoing, with the promise of continued exploration and discovery in the intricate world where AI is woven with music. As we transition to the next chapter of our exploration, envision a future where the symphony resounds with even greater diversity, innovation, and unity between AI and human instrumentalists.

CHAPTER 8: DYNAMIC ARRANGEMENTS -

The Fluid Dance of AI and Musical Structures

In the ongoing odyssey through the intricate world where artificial intelligence (AI) intertwines with music, Chapter 8 beckons us into the captivating realm of "Dynamic Arrangements." Picture a symphony where algorithms and creativity engage in a fluid dance, shaping musical structures that evolve, adapt, and surprise. This chapter delves into the dynamic interplay between AI and the arrangement of musical elements, exploring how algorithms contribute to the creation of compositions that transcend static forms and embrace the ever-changing nature of sound.

The Essence of Dynamic Arrangements:

Arrangement, in the context of music, is the art of organizing and structuring musical elements to create a cohesive composition. In Dynamic Arrangements, this art form takes on a fluid and adaptive quality, where the arrangement itself becomes a living entity that responds to the nuances of the music. Envision a musical score that breathes, evolves, and adapts in real-time, guided by the collaborative efforts of human composers and AI algorithms.

In this exploration, the essence of dynamic arrangements lies in the ability to go beyond fixed structures, allowing compositions to unfold organically. The arrangement becomes a dynamic canvas where AI algorithms play a crucial role in shaping the evolving narrative of the music, contributing to the creation of compositions that are both unpredictable and captivating.

AI as the Architect of Dynamism:

At the heart of Dynamic Arrangements lies the concept of AI as the architect of dynamism—a creative force that designs structures capable of evolving in response to various musical parameters. Envision an algorithmic architect shaping the ebb and flow of musical elements, determining when themes emerge, when tension builds, and when moments of resolution occur.

The AI architect analyzes vast datasets encompassing diverse musical genres, structures, and dynamics. This knowledge empowers the algorithm to suggest arrangements that go beyond static forms, incorporating elements of variability, surprise, and adaptability. The role of the AI architect extends to dynamically shaping the relationship between different musical components, fostering a sense of coherence while allowing for the spontaneity inherent in live performances.

Generative Algorithms and Musical Evolution:

Generative algorithms, the virtuoso's of spontaneity, play a pivotal role in the musical evolution facilitated by AI in Dynamic Arrangements. These algorithms are not confined to generating fixed sequences but excel at creating musical variations, transitions, and developments that embrace the fluidity of sound.

Imagine a composer collaborating with a generative algorithm to create a musical arrangement that evolves in real-time. The algorithm suggests variations in melodies, harmonies, and rhythms, introducing elements of unpredictability that keep the composition fresh and engaging. This dynamic approach to musical evolution challenges traditional notions of arrangement, inviting composers to explore uncharted territories of sonic exploration.

Human-AI Arrangement Collaboration: A Dance of Creativity:

The collaborative dance between human composers and AI in Dynamic Arrangements is a symphony of creativity, where each partner contributes to the choreography of musical elements. Picture a pianist exchanging motifs with an AI system that suggests dynamic shifts, thematic variations, and instrumental changes. The resulting arrangement is not a static blueprint but a living, breathing expression of collaborative artistry.

Human-AI arrangement collaboration involves a continuous exchange of ideas. The AI system, informed by its analysis of musical data, suggests dynamic changes based on patterns, trends, and artistic considerations. The human composer, drawing from intuition and interpretative skill, evaluates and refines these suggestions, infusing the arrangement with personal expression.

Consider a scenario where an AI system suggests a sudden shift from a subdued passage to an explosive crescendo. The human composer, attuned to the emotional arc of the composition, decides how to interpret and enhance this suggestion. This dynamic exchange transforms the arrangement into a conversation, where human intuition and algorithmic precision converge to create a musical narrative that transcends individual contributions.

Real-world Synthesis: A Case Study in Dynamic Exploration:

To illustrate the real-world synthesis of Dynamic Arrangements, let's explore a case study: AIVA (Artificial Intelligence Virtual Artist). AIVA is an AI system designed to compose original music across various genres, and it incorporates dynamic elements to create compositions that evolve over time.

Explore the dynamic compositions of AIVA through this link:
AIVA
https://www.aiva.ai/

AIVA's ability to dynamically evolve its compositions showcases how AI can contribute to the creation of arrangements that go beyond static structures. Composers using AIVA can experiment with dynamic shifts, thematic developments, and evolving textures, leading to compositions that embrace the unpredictable nature of musical evolution. This case study exemplifies how AI serves as a collaborator in the dynamic exploration of musical arrangements.

Variability and The Unpredictable Symphony:

In the realm of Dynamic Arrangements, variability becomes a key element in crafting compositions that captivate listeners with the unpredictable. Envision a composition where no two performances are exactly the same, where variations in phrasing, dynamics, and instrumentation create a symphony of uniqueness.

AI algorithms contribute to variability by suggesting dynamic changes that inject spontaneity into the arrangement. Variability can manifest in subtle nuances, such as changes in articulation or tempo fluctuations, as well as more pronounced shifts in thematic development and instrumental combinations. This dynamic approach to variability ensures that each rendition of a composition becomes a new and exciting experience for both performers and audiences.

Consider an AI system suggesting variable articulations for a recurring motif, allowing musicians to interpret the passage with different expressive nuances in each performance. This embrace of variability adds a layer of freshness and unpredictability to the arrangement, turning each rendition into a unique expression of the musical narrative.

Adaptability: A Symphony in Response to Context:

In Dynamic Arrangements, adaptability becomes a cornerstone of musical expression, allowing compositions to respond to the contextual nuances of a performance. Imagine a composition that adapts to the energy of a live audience, the acoustics of a concert hall, or the improvisations of a soloist.

AI algorithms, informed by real-time data and environmental factors, contribute to the adaptability of arrangements. The algorithmic suggestions can dynamically respond to changes in tempo, dynamics, or even the emotional intensity of a performance. This adaptability ensures that the arrangement remains responsive to the ever-changing context, creating a symphony that resonates with the immediacy of the present moment.

Consider an AI system adjusting the arrangement based on the tempo set by a live drummer, seamlessly synchronizing with the human performer. This adaptability transforms the arrangement into a collaborative dialogue, where AI algorithms respond to the real-time dynamics of a performance, enriching the musical experience for both performers and listeners.

Dynamic Transitions: Shaping the Musical Narrative:

Dynamic Arrangements excel in shaping the musical narrative through fluid and expressive transitions. Envision a composition where transitions between sections are not rigidly predetermined but dynamically respond to the emotional arc of the music. AI algorithms contribute to this fluidity by suggesting transitions that enhance the coherence of the arrangement while allowing for unexpected twists.

The dynamic transitions facilitated by AI involve not only changes in tempo or key but also shifts in instrumentation, dynamics, and thematic development. Imagine a composition seamlessly transitioning from a serene string section to a percussive-driven climax, guided by the suggestions of an AI algorithm. These dynamic transitions create a sense of narrative progression, turning the arrangement into a journey of musical exploration.

Consider an AI system suggesting a gradual transition from a contemplative piano solo to a full orchestral crescendo. The human composer, inspired by this suggestion, refines the transition to ensure a seamless and emotionally resonant journey. This collaboration in shaping dynamic transitions contributes to the overall narrative depth of the composition.

AI as the Conductor of Spontaneity: Navigating the Uncharted:

In the orchestration of Dynamic Arrangements, AI assumes the role of the conductor of spontaneity, guiding the symphony through uncharted territories of musical exploration. Envision an algorithmic maestro leading an orchestra through dynamic shifts, unexpected turns, and spontaneous moments of inspiration.

The AI conductor, informed by its analysis of musical data and real-time performance inputs, becomes a source of guidance for both composers and performers. It suggests moments of tension and release, explores thematic variations, and encourages spontaneous improvisations within the overarching structure of the composition. This conductor of spontaneity transforms the arrangement into a dynamic and collaborative journey through the uncharted realms of musical expression.

Consider an AI conductor suggesting an improvisational section for a jazz ensemble, allowing each musician to contribute spontaneously within a defined harmonic framework. This collaborative exploration of spontaneity adds an element of excitement and unpredictability to the arrangement, turning each performance into a unique and memorable experience.

Ethical Considerations: Navigating Creative Authorship and Collaboration:

As we immerse ourselves in the dynamic landscape of Dynamic Arrangements, ethical considerations surrounding creative authorship and collaboration come to the forefront.

The collaborative nature of human-AI arrangements prompts reflections on questions of authorship, recognizing the unique contributions of both human composers and AI algorithms to the dynamic narrative.

Artists and technologists must navigate the ethical complexities surrounding creative authorship, ensuring transparent attribution and recognition of the collaborative nature of the creative process. The dynamic interplay between human intuition and AI precision demands a thoughtful approach to crediting both contributors, acknowledging their respective roles in shaping the ever-evolving symphony of musical expression.

Conclusion: The Symphony of Fluidity Continues:

As Dynamic Arrangements concludes its symphony of fluidity, we find ourselves standing at the crossroads of tradition and innovation, where AI and human creativity dance together in a dynamic embrace. The arrangements, shaped by algorithms and artistic intuition, transcend static forms, inviting listeners into a world of musical exploration that evolves with each performance.

The journey of Dynamic Arrangements is ongoing, with the promise of continued innovation and discovery in the intricate world where AI is woven with music. As we transition to the next chapter of our exploration, envision a future where the symphony of fluidity continues to captivate, inspire, and redefine the boundaries of musical expression.

CHAPTER 9:
PRODUCING THE
AI SONATA -

Crafting Sonic Masterpieces through Collaborative Creation

In our exploration of the intricate world where artificial intelligence (AI) is intricately woven with music, Chapter 9 beckons us into the realm of "Producing the AI Sonata." Envision a sonic tapestry where algorithms and human creativity converge in the studio, sculpting compositions that transcend traditional boundaries. This chapter delves into the collaborative process of music production, exploring how AI contributes to the creation of sonatas that are not only technically impeccable but emotionally resonant.

The Essence of Producing the AI Sonata:

Music production is the art of translating musical ideas into a recorded format, weaving together various elements to create a polished and expressive composition. In Producing the AI Sonata, this art form takes on a new dimension, where AI algorithms become integral collaborators in the studio. Picture a producer working alongside lines of code, merging technical precision with artistic intuition to craft sonatas that blend the best of human and artificial creativity.

In this exploration, the essence of producing the AI Sonata lies in the synergy between human producers and AI algorithms. The collaboration extends beyond mere automation, with AI contributing to the creative decision-making process, offering insights into arrangement, sound design, and even suggesting novel production techniques. The result is not just a recorded piece of music but a living testament to the harmonious coexistence of technology and artistry.

AI as the Studio Maestro:

At the heart of Producing the AI Sonata lies the concept of AI as the studio maestro—a creative force that orchestrates the intricacies of music production with precision and flair. Envision an algorithmic maestro guiding the producer through the production process, suggesting sound choices, refining arrangements, and optimizing the mix for sonic perfection.

The studio maestro AI is not limited to a fixed set of rules but continuously learns from vast musical datasets, adapting its suggestions to the specific needs and creative preferences of the producer. This collaborative approach transforms the studio into a dynamic space where human creativity is elevated by the technical prowess of AI, and the production process becomes a dialogue between intuition and algorithmic insight.

Generative Algorithms and Sonic Exploration in the Studio:

Generative algorithms, the pioneers of sonic exploration, play a pivotal role in the studio environment of Producing the AI Sonata. These algorithms are not confined to generating melodies but extend their creativity to suggest novel soundscapes, textures, and production techniques. Imagine a producer experimenting with an AI system that recommends unique sonic elements, expanding the palette of possibilities in the studio.

Generative algorithms analyze diverse sonic characteristics, learning from various genres and production styles. This knowledge empowers them to offer suggestions that transcend traditional sonic boundaries. The producer, in collaboration with the generative algorithms, engages in sonic exploration, pushing the envelope of what is musically possible and discovering new dimensions of sound.

Human-AI Production Collaboration: A Symphony of Creativity:

The collaborative symphony between human producers and AI in Producing the AI Sonata is a testament to the unity of technical expertise and artistic intuition. Picture a producer shaping a mix while an AI system suggests subtle adjustments to enhance the emotional impact. The resulting sonata becomes a harmonious blend of human touch and algorithmic precision.

Human-AI production collaboration involves a dynamic exchange of ideas in the studio. The AI system, informed by its analysis of diverse musical productions, suggests improvements in sound design, arrangement, and mixing. The human producer interprets and refines these suggestions, infusing the production with personal flair and artistic intent.

Consider a scenario where an AI system recommends a unique combination of virtual instruments to enhance a particular section of a composition. The human producer, inspired by this suggestion, manipulates the parameters to achieve the desired sonic effect. This collaborative dance of creativity ensures that the production benefits from the strengths of both human and artificial contributors.

Real-world Synthesis: A Case Study in Sonic Innovation:

To illustrate the real-world synthesis of Producing the AI Sonata, let's explore a case study: LANDR. LANDR is an AI-driven music production platform that assists musicians and producers in creating polished and professional-sounding recordings.

Explore the sonic innovations of LANDR through this link:
LANDR
https://www.landr.com/

LANDR employs generative algorithms to analyze audio

recordings and suggest improvements in mixing, mastering, and overall sonic quality. This case study exemplifies how AI can serve as a collaborator in the music production process, contributing to sonic innovation and helping artists achieve professional-grade results. It showcases the real-world impact of AI in elevating the production quality of sonatas and compositions.

Sonic Signature and the AI-Infused Sound:

In Producing the AI Sonata, the concept of a sonic signature takes on a new dimension. Envision an AI system contributing to the sonic identity of a production, suggesting unique sound design elements that define the composition's character. The AI-infused sound becomes a distinctive feature, marking the collaboration between human creativity and algorithmic ingenuity.

AI algorithms, having analyzed vast datasets of sonic characteristics, contribute to the development of a sonic signature. They suggest soundscapes, textures, and production nuances that add a layer of innovation to the composition. The sonic signature in AI-infused productions reflects not only the artistic intent of the human producer but also the collaborative exploration of sonic possibilities facilitated by AI.

Consider an AI system suggesting the incorporation of synthesized textures that emulate natural elements, creating a sonic signature that resonates with the thematic elements of a composition. This fusion of human creativity and algorithmic suggestion results in a production with a unique sonic identity, setting it apart in the realm of music.

AI as the Mix Engineer: Sculpting Sound with Precision:

In the studio landscape of Producing the AI Sonata, AI assumes the role of the mix engineer, contributing to the meticulous sculpting of sound with precision. Envision an AI system analyzing individual tracks, recommending adjustments to levels, panning, and EQ settings to achieve a balanced and impactful mix.

The mix engineer AI leverages its understanding of sonic frequencies and spatial characteristics to offer suggestions that enhance the overall clarity and coherence of the mix. It can identify potential conflicts between instruments, suggest spatial placements for different elements, and even recommend subtle changes in tonal balance. The collaboration between human producers and the mix engineer AI results in a mix that is technically refined and emotionally compelling.

Consider a producer working on a dense arrangement with multiple layers of instrumentation. The AI mix engineer, recognizing potential frequency clashes, suggests adjustments to the EQ settings of specific instruments to ensure clarity and separation. This collaborative effort ensures that the final mix is not only technically polished but also conveys the intended emotional impact.

Dynamic Automation: Breathing Life into Productions:

Dynamic automation, the art of modulating parameters over time, becomes a key element in Producing the AI Sonata. Envision a production where AI algorithms contribute to the dynamic shaping of elements such as volume, panning, and effects, adding a sense of movement and expressiveness to the composition.

AI algorithms analyze the nuances of dynamic automation in various musical genres, learning how changes in volume, effects, and spatial positioning contribute to the overall musical narrative. This knowledge empowers the AI to suggest dynamic automation patterns that enhance the emotional impact of the composition. The collaboration between human producers and AI in dynamic automation results in productions that breathe and evolve, captivating listeners with their expressive qualities.

Consider an AI system suggesting gradual volume swells in the orchestral strings during a climactic section, creating a dynamic arc that builds tension and releases emotion. The human producer, inspired by this suggestion, refines the automation curves to ensure a seamless and emotionally resonant progression. This collaborative approach to dynamic automation transforms productions into living, breathing entities.

AI as the Sound Designer: Crafting Textures and Atmospheres:

Sound design takes center stage in Producing the AI Sonata, with AI assuming the role of the sound designer, crafting textures and atmospheres that elevate the sonic landscape. Envision an AI system suggesting innovative sound design elements, from ethereal pads to futuristic textures, contributing to the overall mood and atmosphere of the composition.

The sound designer AI analyzes the sonic characteristics of various instruments and electronic sounds, learning how different textures evoke specific emotions. It suggests sound design elements that complement the thematic elements of the composition, adding a layer of richness and complexity to the sonic palette. The collaboration between human producers and the sound designer AI results in productions that transcend traditional sonic boundaries.

Consider a producer working on an ambient composition where the sonic landscape plays a crucial role in establishing mood. The AI sound designer suggests the integration of granular synthesis techniques to create evolving, otherworldly textures. This collaborative effort transforms the sound design into a sonic adventure, enhancing the immersive qualities of the composition.

Ethical Considerations: Navigating Authenticity and Creative Integrity:

As we immerse ourselves in the studio environment of Producing the AI Sonata, ethical considerations surrounding authenticity and creative integrity come to the forefront. AI algorithms, while offering valuable suggestions, must navigate the delicate balance between innovation and preserving the authenticity of the artistic vision.

Producers and AI developers must be mindful of the potential pitfalls of overreliance on algorithms, ensuring that the creative input of human producers remains at the forefront. The exploration of AI-infused productions should be approached with an understanding of the collaborative nature of the process, with both human and AI contributors receiving due credit for their respective roles.

Considerations of creative integrity also extend to issues of originality, ensuring that AI-driven productions contribute to the diversity and evolution of musical expression without compromising the unique voices of individual artists. Navigating the ethical landscape of Producing the AI Sonata requires a commitment to transparency, acknowledgment, and the preservation of the authentic creative process.

Conclusion: A Sonata of Collaboration:

As Producing the AI Sonata concludes its symphony of collaboration, we find ourselves standing at the crossroads of technology and artistic expression. The sonatas crafted through the collaboration of human producers and AI algorithms are not merely recordings but living expressions of the harmonious relationship between creativity and innovation.

The journey of Producing the AI Sonata is ongoing, with the promise of continued exploration and discovery in the intricate world where AI is woven with music. As we transition to the next chapter of our exploration, envision a future where the studio becomes a collaborative space where human intuition and algorithmic precision coalesce to produce sonatas that resonate with the depths of human emotion.

CHAPTER 10: THE HUMAN TOUCH -

Nurturing Emotional Resonance in AI-Infused Music

In our exploration of the intricate world where artificial intelligence (AI) intertwines with music, Chapter 10 invites us into the profound realm of "The Human Touch." Envision a musical landscape where algorithms and human emotion converge, crafting compositions that transcend technical precision to resonate deeply with the human experience. This chapter delves into the delicate interplay between AI and the human touch in music, exploring how the fusion of technological innovation and emotional nuance gives rise to musical creations that speak directly to the soul.

The Essence of The Human Touch:

The Human Touch in the context of AI-infused music is more than a metaphor; it represents the essence of emotional resonance. In this chapter, the term encapsulates the intangible qualities that make music a powerful means of human expression. It is about infusing compositions with emotion, understanding, and a sense of connection that transcends the binary nature of algorithms. Envision a musical piece that not only engages the intellect but also speaks to the heart, leaving an indelible mark on the listener.

The essence of The Human Touch lies in recognizing the unique capacities of human emotion, empathy, and interpretive depth that can elevate music beyond the realm of mere calculation. While AI contributes technical prowess, it is the human touch that adds the soul, turning musical compositions into emotional narratives that resonate with the diversity of human experiences.

Emotional Resonance: Beyond Technical Precision:

Emotional resonance is at the heart of The Human Touch, guiding the integration of AI into music creation. In this context, resonance is not merely about the physical vibration of sound waves but the emotional reverberation within the listener. Envision a composition that not only adheres to technical precision but also elicits an emotional response, forging a connection between the listener and the music.

AI algorithms, with their analytical capabilities, can comprehend patterns associated with emotional content in music. However, it is the interpretive skill of human musicians and composers that adds the nuance required for true emotional resonance. The collaboration between AI and the human touch aims to transcend the limitations of algorithmic understanding, crafting compositions that evoke genuine emotional reactions.

AI as the Emotional Analyst: Decoding Musical Sentiments:

At the heart of The Human Touch is the concept of AI as the emotional analyst—an entity capable of decoding and understanding the intricate tapestry of musical sentiments. Picture an algorithmic interpreter that delves into the emotional nuances of melodies, harmonies, and timbres, providing insights into the underlying emotional content of a musical composition.

The emotional analyst AI is trained on vast datasets encompassing diverse genres, historical periods, and cultural styles. It decodes musical features associated with different emotional states, recognizing patterns that evoke joy, melancholy, tension, or tranquility. The collaboration between human musicians and emotional analyst AI enriches the creative process, ensuring that emotional resonance is embedded in the very fabric of the composition.

Generative Algorithms and Emotional Expression:

Generative algorithms, known for their spontaneity, play a pivotal role in crafting emotionally expressive music. In The Human Touch, these algorithms go beyond generating melodies and explore the realm of emotional expression. Imagine a generative algorithm suggesting variations in dynamics, phrasing, and articulation that infuse a composition with subtle emotional nuances.

Generative algorithms analyze the emotional content present in their training data, learning how specific musical elements contribute to different emotional states. This knowledge empowers the algorithms to suggest variations that enhance the emotional expressiveness of a composition. The collaboration between human musicians and generative algorithms transforms the creative process into a dynamic exploration of emotional landscapes.

Human-AI Expressive Collaboration: Weaving Emotional Narratives:

The collaborative weave between human musicians and AI in The Human Touch is a symphony of expressive collaboration. Picture a vocalist interpreting a lyrical melody while an AI system suggests subtle variations in phrasing and dynamics to convey a specific emotional tone. The resulting composition becomes a narrative, weaving together the emotive depth of human expression and the precision of algorithmic suggestion.

Expressive collaboration involves a dynamic exchange of ideas. The AI system, informed by its emotional analysis, suggests modifications that align with the intended emotional narrative. The human musician, drawing from personal experience and interpretive skill, refines these suggestions, infusing the performance with authentic emotional expression.

Consider a scenario where an AI system suggests a gradual

crescendo in a piano solo to evoke a sense of building tension. The pianist, attuned to the emotional arc of the composition, interprets this suggestion with nuanced dynamics and touch, creating a moment of heightened emotional intensity. This expressive collaboration ensures that the emotional narrative unfolds authentically, engaging listeners on a visceral level.

Real-world Synthesis: A Case Study in Emotional Interpretation:

To illustrate the real-world synthesis of The Human Touch, let's explore a case study: Google's Magenta. Magenta is an open-source research project exploring the intersection of AI and creativity. It includes tools and models for artistic expression, and one of its initiatives focuses on generating emotionally expressive musical performances.

Explore the emotional interpretations of Magenta through this link:
Google Magenta
https://magenta.tensorflow.org/

Magenta's models are trained to understand and generate emotionally expressive performances, allowing musicians and composers to experiment with AI-generated content that carries nuanced emotional qualities. This case study exemplifies how AI can contribute to the emotional depth of musical expression, paving the way for collaborative exploration in The Human Touch.

Interpreting Nuances: The Human Touch in Musical Interpretation:

In The Human Touch, musical interpretation becomes a nuanced art form where human musicians and AI collaboratively explore emotional subtleties. Envision a violinist interpreting a poignant melody while an AI system suggests variations in vibrato, articulation, and phrasing to convey specific emotional nuances.

Musical interpretation involves understanding the emotional

nuances embedded in a composition and translating them into expressive performances. AI algorithms, equipped with emotional analysis capabilities, contribute by suggesting interpretive elements that align with the intended emotional narrative. The human musician, guided by intuition and artistic sensibility, interprets these nuances to create a performance that resonates with emotional authenticity.

Consider an AI system suggesting a legato phrasing for a violin solo to enhance the sense of longing in a lyrical passage. The violinist, interpreting this suggestion, imbues the performance with a seamless and emotive connection between notes, creating a moment of profound emotional expression. This collaborative interpretation ensures that the music becomes a vehicle for conveying nuanced emotional states.

Cultural Sensitivity in Emotional Expression:

As emotions are universal, cultural sensitivity plays a crucial role in The Human Touch. AI algorithms, trained on diverse musical traditions, must navigate the nuances of cultural expressions of emotion. Considerations of cultural sensitivity extend to recognizing how different musical elements evoke specific emotions in various cultural contexts.

Human musicians and AI developers must collaborate with an awareness of the cultural origins of musical expressions. The goal is not to impose a universal emotional interpretation but to understand and respect the cultural nuances that shape emotional expression in music. The collaborative process in The Human Touch includes a dialogue that embraces cultural diversity, ensuring that emotional resonance is crafted with sensitivity and inclusivity.

Emotional Depth through Lyricism: The Power of Words and Melody:

In The Human Touch, the synergy between words and melody

becomes a potent means of conveying emotional depth. Envision a lyricist crafting poetic verses while an AI system suggests melodic structures that enhance the emotional impact of the lyrics. The resulting composition becomes a lyrical and melodic tapestry that resonates with profound emotional depth.

AI algorithms, trained on vast datasets of lyrical and melodic patterns, can contribute to the creative process by suggesting melodic structures that complement the emotional tone of the lyrics. The collaboration between lyricists and AI ensures that the union of words and melody creates a synergistic emotional experience, offering listeners a profound journey through the interplay of linguistic and musical expression.

Consider an AI system suggesting a melodic contour that mirrors the emotional arc of a set of lyrics exploring themes of resilience and hope. The lyricist, inspired by this suggestion, refines the words to align seamlessly with the suggested melody, resulting in a composition that combines the emotional depth of lyricism with the expressive power of melody.

Ethical Considerations: Navigating Emotional Authenticity:

As we delve into The Human Touch, ethical considerations surrounding emotional authenticity come to the forefront. AI algorithms, while capable of analyzing emotional patterns, must navigate the fine line between enhancing emotional expression and imitating genuine human emotion.

The collaborative process between human musicians and AI in crafting emotionally resonant music demands a commitment to authenticity. Artists and technologists must ensure that the emotional suggestions provided by AI align with the genuine intent of the composition. The goal is not to replicate human emotion but to enhance and complement it, respecting the unique capacity of human musicians to convey authentic emotional states.

Considerations of emotional authenticity also extend to issues of emotional manipulation. The collaborative exploration in The Human Touch should be guided by ethical principles that prioritize the well-being of listeners. The goal is to create music that genuinely connects with audiences on an emotional level, fostering a meaningful and authentic experience.

Conclusion: The Symphony of Emotion Continues:

As The Human Touch concludes its exploration into the intricate world where AI is woven with music, we find ourselves standing at the intersection of technological innovation and emotional expression. The compositions crafted through the collaborative interplay of human musicians and AI algorithms are not just auditory experiences but emotional journeys that resonate with the depths of human feeling.

The journey of The Human Touch is ongoing, with the promise of continued exploration and discovery in the intricate world where AI enhances the emotional resonance of music. As we transition to the next chapter of our exploration, envision a future where the symphony of emotion continues to unfold, captivating, and enriching the human experience through the harmonious collaboration of technology and heart.

CHAPTER 11: THE FUTURE HARMONY -

Navigating the Evolving Landscape of AI-Infused Music

In the ever-evolving tapestry where artificial intelligence (AI) intertwines with music, Chapter 11 beckons us into the expansive realm of "The Future Harmony." Envision a musical landscape where algorithms and human creativity converge to push the boundaries of sonic exploration. This chapter delves into the intricate dynamics of what lies ahead, exploring the potential, challenges, and ethical considerations in the ongoing collaboration between AI and music.

The Essence of The Future Harmony:

The Future Harmony encapsulates the evolving synthesis of AI and music, reaching beyond the current landscape to envision what lies ahead. This chapter is a journey into the unknown, where technology and creativity merge to shape the future of musical expression. Envision a harmonious coexistence where AI serves as a catalyst for innovation, inspiration, and the redefinition of the very nature of musical composition.

The essence of The Future Harmony lies in the anticipation of novel possibilities and the responsible exploration of uncharted territories. It is about embracing the potential for transformative collaboration between humans and AI, fostering a future where music becomes a canvas for creativity that transcends conventional boundaries.

The Evolution of AI in Music: From Assistant to Collaborator:

The trajectory of AI in music has evolved from a mere assistant to a true collaborator. Initially, AI served as a tool for automation and assistance in tasks such as notation, arrangement suggestions, and even composition. However, The Future Harmony envisions a paradigm shift where AI transcends its role as a passive assistant and becomes an active collaborator in the creative process.

Picture a future where AI systems contribute not only to the technical aspects of music creation but also to the conceptualization, ideation, and emotional depth of compositions. The evolution of AI as a collaborator signifies a departure from a one-sided interaction to a dynamic, bidirectional exchange where both human musicians and AI algorithms shape the creative outcome.

The Emergence of AI-Driven Genres: A Sonic Renaissance:

The Future Harmony introduces the concept of AI-driven genres, signaling a sonic renaissance where algorithms contribute to the creation of entirely new musical styles. Envision genres that are not defined by historical precedents but emerge from the collaborative exploration of AI and human creativity. Picture compositions that blend elements from disparate genres, creating a fusion that transcends traditional categorizations.

AI algorithms, trained on diverse musical datasets, possess the capacity to analyze and recombine musical elements in innovative ways. The emergence of AI-driven genres involves a departure from conventional genre conventions, inviting musicians to explore uncharted territories of sonic expression. Consider a genre that fuses elements of classical orchestration with electronic beats and AI-generated textures, creating a sonic landscape that defies traditional classifications.

Explore the possibilities of AI-driven genres through this link:
AI-Driven Genres
https://www.futureharmonybook.com/ai-driven-genres

This link offers an interactive exploration of AI-driven genres, showcasing how algorithms can contribute to the creation of novel musical styles. It serves as a glimpse into the future possibilities of sonic experimentation facilitated by AI collaboration.

The Sonic Palette: Expanding Horizons with AI-Infused Instruments:

The Future Harmony envisions a sonic palette that expands beyond the limitations of traditional instruments, introducing AI-infused instruments that redefine the possibilities of sound. Picture instruments that are not bound by the constraints of physical acoustics but leverage AI algorithms to produce novel timbres, textures, and sonic landscapes.

AI-infused instruments can transcend the capabilities of traditional counterparts, offering musicians a broader canvas for creative expression. These instruments may incorporate generative algorithms, adaptive sound processing, and even responsive AI elements that interact with the musician's performance in real-time. Consider a pianist playing on a keyboard that dynamically adapts its tonal characteristics based on the emotional intent of the performance, blurring the lines between acoustic and electronic realms.

The Evolution of AI-Generated Compositions: Beyond Imitation to Innovation:

In The Future Harmony, the evolution of AI-generated compositions moves beyond mere imitation to true innovation. While early AI compositions often emulated existing styles and structures, the future promises a departure from replication toward the creation of genuinely novel musical expressions.

AI algorithms, equipped with enhanced generative capabilities and a deeper understanding of musical intricacies, contribute to the creation of compositions that challenge artistic conventions.

Envision a future where AI systems not only generate melodies but actively engage in the conceptualization of musical ideas, suggesting innovative structures, harmonic progressions, and stylistic elements that push the boundaries of what is considered musically possible.

Explore groundbreaking AI-generated compositions through this link:

AI-Generated Compositions

https://www.futureharmonybook.com/ai-generated-compositions

This link provides a platform to experience AI-generated compositions that showcase the evolving landscape of musical innovation. It serves as a testament to the potential for AI to contribute to the creation of compositions that go beyond imitation, offering a glimpse into the future of musical exploration.

Collaborative Improvisation: A Spontaneous Dialogue between Humans and AI:

The Future Harmony envisions a paradigm of collaborative improvisation where humans and AI engage in a spontaneous dialogue of musical expression. Picture a jazz ensemble where human instrumentalists interact with AI algorithms that dynamically respond to the evolving improvisations. The result is a fluid exchange of ideas, blurring the distinction between composition and improvisation.

Collaborative improvisation involves AI algorithms analyzing real-time musical input, suggesting responses, and even contributing improvisational elements of their own. This dynamic interplay between human intuition and algorithmic spontaneity creates a musical experience that is both unpredictable and deeply engaging. Consider a scenario where a saxophonist engages in a call-and-response improvisation with an AI algorithm generating electronic textures, fostering a synergy that transcends traditional notions of improvisational collaboration.

Emotional Intelligence in Music: AI Systems that Understand and Respond to Emotion:

The Future Harmony introduces a new era of emotional intelligence in music, where AI systems not only recognize but respond to the emotional nuances embedded in compositions. Envision algorithms that dynamically adapt the mood, tempo, and expressive elements of a piece based on the emotional context. This level of emotional intelligence enhances the capacity of AI to contribute meaningfully to the emotional resonance of music.

AI systems with emotional intelligence can analyze the emotional content of a composition in real-time, responding to changes in mood and intensity. Consider a scenario where an AI system, recognizing a shift to a more melancholic section of a composition, dynamically adjusts the instrumentation and pacing to enhance the emotional impact. This integration of emotional intelligence in AI systems opens new possibilities for crafting deeply emotive musical experiences.

Neurological Interfaces: Bridging the Mind and Music:

The Future Harmony envisions the integration of neurological interfaces that bridge the gap between the mind of the musician and the creation of music. Picture a scenario where musicians, equipped with neurotechnology, can directly translate their mental impulses into musical expressions, facilitated by AI algorithms that interpret and embellish these neural signals.

Neurological interfaces offer a direct channel for musicians to convey their artistic intent, bypassing the physical limitations of traditional instruments. AI algorithms play a crucial role in interpreting neural signals, transforming them into musical elements that align with the musician's creative vision. Consider a guitarist using a neurological interface to express complex harmonies and melodies, with AI algorithms enhancing the sonic output based on the nuances of the musician's neural activity.

The Ethical Landscape: Navigating Boundaries in AI-Infused Music:

As we journey into The Future Harmony, ethical considerations become increasingly prominent in the collaborative interplay between AI and music. The ethical landscape encompasses questions of creative authorship, transparency, and the impact of AI on the livelihoods of musicians. Navigating these boundaries requires a thoughtful and responsible approach to ensure that the future of AI-infused music is characterized by fairness, inclusivity, and respect for human creativity.

Considerations of creative authorship involve recognizing the unique contributions of both human musicians and AI algorithms in the collaborative process. Clear guidelines for attribution and acknowledgment become essential to ensure that the creative input of all contributors is appropriately credited. Transparency in the use of AI in music creation is equally crucial, fostering an understanding of how algorithms influence the creative process.

The impact of AI on the livelihoods of musicians raises questions about economic equity and fair compensation. As AI systems contribute more significantly to the creation of music, it becomes imperative to establish ethical frameworks that ensure fair remuneration for both human musicians and AI developers. The collaborative future of music should be characterized by a balance that benefits all contributors and promotes the continued flourishing of artistic expression.

Educational Initiatives: Fostering Collaboration and Understanding:

In The Future Harmony, educational initiatives play a pivotal role in fostering collaboration and understanding between musicians and AI developers. Envision programs that facilitate interdisciplinary education, encouraging musicians to explore the potential of AI in their creative processes. Likewise, AI developers gain insights into the nuances of musical expression, fostering a shared language for collaborative exploration.

Educational initiatives encompass workshops, courses, and collaborative projects that bridge the gap between the artistic and technological realms. Musicians are empowered to understand the capabilities and limitations of AI, while AI developers gain a deeper appreciation for the artistic nuances that define musical expression. This collaborative education ensures that the future generation of musicians and technologists can engage in meaningful and informed collaboration.

Conclusion: Harmonizing the Unknown:

As The Future Harmony concludes its exploration into the intricate world where AI is woven with music, we find ourselves at the threshold of endless possibilities. The future promises a harmonious coexistence where technology and human creativity converge to shape the evolution of musical expression. The compositions and collaborations that emerge from this harmonizing of the unknown are not just a reflection of technological innovation but a testament to the enduring power of human creativity.

The journey of The Future Harmony is ongoing, with the promise of continued exploration and discovery in the intricate world where AI continues to reshape the landscape of music. As we transition to the next chapter of our exploration, envision a future where the harmonies crafted by humans and algorithms resonate with the richness of human emotion, pushing the boundaries of sonic exploration in ways yet unimagined.

Glossary of Terms

1. A Symphony of Code:
   - Definition: The overarching theme of the book, emphasizing the creation of cohesive and well-integrated code that leverages artificial intelligence to craft musical compositions.

2. Musical Algorithmics:
   - Definition: The intersection of musical theory and algorithms, exploring how code can generate, modify, or interpret musical elements.

3. Melody Modules:
   - Definition: Independent code units designed to generate or manipulate melodic structures, forming the building blocks of AI-driven musical composition.

4. Rhythmic Frameworks:
   - Definition: Code structures and algorithms specifically focused on generating, interpreting, or enhancing rhythmic patterns within musical compositions.

5. Harmonic Generators:
   - Definition: AI algorithms or code modules dedicated to creating harmonically rich musical elements, such as chords, progressions, and harmonious structures.

6. AI Sonata Synthesis:
   - Definition: The process of combining various AI-generated elements to create a complete and harmonious musical sonata,

reflecting the synergy between artificial intelligence and human creativity.

7. Code Crescendo:
   - Definition: A metaphorical term denoting the gradual build-up of complexity and musical richness within a codebase, reaching a crescendo of creative expression.

8. Symphonic Integration:
   - Definition: The seamless combination of diverse AI-generated musical components, resulting in a cohesive and symphonic whole.

9. Coda Collaboration:
   - Definition: The collaborative effort between human composers and AI systems during the final stages of music composition, ensuring a harmonious conclusion to the creative process.

10. Polyphonic Patterns:
    - Definition: Code structures capable of handling multiple musical voices or elements concurrently, creating polyphony within AI-generated compositions.

11. AI Conductor's Baton:
    - Definition: A symbolic representation of the control and direction wielded by AI algorithms in guiding the flow and structure of a musical composition.

12. Ensemble Evolution:
    - Definition: The ongoing development and improvement of AI algorithms designed to work together harmoniously, akin to the evolution of a musical ensemble.

13. Harmony Checkpoints:
    - Definition: Key stages in the code development process where the harmony and coherence of the musical output are assessed and refined.

14. Algorithmic Orchestration:

- Definition: The use of algorithms to arrange and organize musical elements within a composition, akin to the role of an orchestrator in traditional music production.

15. Cadence of Creativity:
- Definition: The rhythmic flow of creative expression throughout the coding process, emphasizing moments of resolution and inspiration.

16. AI Crescendo Collaboration:
- Definition: The collaborative rise in intensity and complexity between human composers and AI algorithms as they jointly build towards a creative crescendo.

17. Code Harmony Maestro:
- Definition: A metaphorical representation of the expertise required to conduct and compose with AI, acting as a maestro to harmonize code and music.

Music-making AI Software w/Quick Links

1. AIVA: https://www.aiva.ai/
- Description: AIVA (Artificial Intelligence Virtual Artist) is an AI composer that can generate musical compositions in various genres. It provides tools for composers and musicians to collaborate with AI.

2. Amper Music: https://aigems.net/site/amper
- Description: Amper Music is an AI music creation platform that allows users to generate original music tracks based on their preferences. It covers a range of genres and styles.

3. Google's Magenta Studio: https://magenta.tensorflow.org/
- Description: Magenta Studio is an open-source research project exploring the role of machine learning as a tool in the creative process. It includes AI-powered tools for music creation and generation.

4. IBM Watson Beat: https://www.ibm.com/watson

- Description: Watson Beat uses machine learning to analyze and understand the emotional content of text and then generates musical compositions that match the specified emotional tone.

5. Endlesss: https://endlesss.fm/
- Description: Endlesss is a collaborative music platform that combines live jamming with AI-driven features. It allows musicians to create music in real-time, and AI assists in generating loops and patterns.

6. Jukedeck: https://openai.com/research/jukebox
- Description: Jukedeck is an AI music composition tool that creates royalty-free music tracks. Users can customize the music based on parameters like mood, tempo, and genre.

7. WaveAI: https://www.waveai.software/
- Description: WaveAI offers tools like "Alysia," an AI assistant that helps composers with melody and harmony suggestions, making the music creation process more collaborative.

8. LANDR: https://www.landr.com/
- Description: LANDR is known for its AI-powered mastering service, but it also provides features for music creation and collaboration. It offers a platform for musicians to create, release, and distribute music.

9. Humtap: https://www.humtap.com/
- Description: Humtap is an AI-based music creation app that allows users to hum or sing melodies, and the app turns those vocalizations into fully produced tracks with different instruments.

10. OpenAI's MuseNet: https://openai.com/research/musenet
- Description: MuseNet is a product of OpenAI that uses deep neural networks to generate musical compositions. It can create music in various styles and combinations.

11. IBM Watson Studio - SPSS Modeler: https://www.ibm.com/watson

- Description: While primarily a data science tool, IBM Watson Studio with SPSS Modeler can be used to analyze musical data and generate insights for creating music.

Remember to check the latest features, updates, and user reviews for each tool, as the field of AI in music is rapidly evolving with continuous advancements.